The
Sacred
Continuum

Our Life between Prayers

Stephanie Sorensen

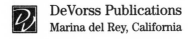

DeVorss Publications
Marina del Rey, California

© 2000 Stephanie Sorensen

ISBN: 0-87516-735-7

Library of Congress Catalog Card Number: 00-130620

DeVorss & Company, *Publishers*
P.O. Box 550
Marina del Rey CA 90294-0550

Printed in the United States of America

Contents

Preface

Is IT POSSIBLE for us to consciously practice *prayer-like* thought in the space between our officially designated prayers? Can we learn to supersede our *every* reaction and response to the material world, as we do in prayer, with a ceaseless acknowledgment of Spirit as the only *true* Source and Substance of all that exists?

Our focus and concern in recognizing Truth is to express It more clearly as individuals and to see It more clearly in the totality of life everywhere. This isn't always easy (though *always* the Truth) because sometimes the connection between Spirit and the world we see is hard to detect. While certain forms and their activities may clearly reflect some aspect of their Originative Divine Cause, others may seem to deny It altogether. It is towards this "closer proximity" that those who practice Spiritual Mind Treatment, Affirmative Prayer, and Creative Meditation aspire.

Ernest Holmes, the founder of Religious Science, suggested the importance of treating or praying twice a day. The purpose of such prayer is to aid in our conscious recognition of, and unification with, Spirit as All-knowing, All-powerful, and Ever-present—and then allow this awareness to guide our thinking along a specific line of realization to the revelation of God-Only behind a particular condition. Dr. Holmes was not suggesting, however, that our conscious awareness of, and adherence to, Truth be allocated to the "official" act of prayer or that between our prayers it matters less what we recognize as present and creative in our lives. He wrote in *Creative Mind:*

> *We cannot make affirmations for fifteen minutes a day and spend the rest of our time denying the things which we have affirmed, and affirming the thing which we have denied, and obtain the results which we seek.*

We live, move and have our being in a Sacred Continuum, an unbroken and inseparable Wholeness which has no beginning or end, no pause or disconnectedness, no separate parts. If we want to reveal the Truth of Being *permanently,* we can't do it by praying *periodically.* The Divine Ear is *always* listening. We are in constant communion with Spirit. We must consciously *live* our prayers and choose our thoughts carefully, moment to moment, if we want to change our lives.

It may seem cumbersome, even tiring, to compel ourselves to be aware of every little thing we're thinking about and speaking of when we are not actively praying. But it is the only way for us to be certain that we are living in alignment with the Truth we speak in our Treatments and Affirmative Prayers rather than negating It.

Learning to do something new or in a different way always seems difficult in the beginning because we must constantly remind ourselves of the correct way to do it—until *that* way becomes *our* way. For example, if we were learning to drive a car, in the beginning it might be necessary for us to frequently remind ourselves which pedal was for gas and which was the brake. We might need to constantly remind ourselves to signal before turning, to look in the rearview mirror before changing lanes, and to yield to the person on our right at a stop sign.

At times these constant reminders might seem frustrating and unnatural. But after a while the flow and movement of driving would become so natural and fluid that we would seldom if ever need to remind ourselves of the proper way to drive. In fact, the act of driving often becomes so natural that we do most of it unconsciously while we carry on a conversation or listen to the radio.

The same process applies to our learning to *live* the Truth we speak of in our prayers. We can choose to drive a car or we can take the bus instead, but we cannot choose whether to think or not. We can, however, learn how to think "correctly" by recognizing Spirit as all, and then consciously choose *what* we will focus on and speak of in our life.

As we learn to think and speak *all of the time* as if we truly know our relationship to that Presence in which we live and move and have our being, we consciously experience the power of our word in every moment. We realize that there is no "in" or "out" to Treatment because we are aware that every thought and word enters into the Creative Medium the moment it occurs, and that *every* thought and word is a prayer.

Introduction

THIS BOOK is about the power of our word—spoken and unspoken—to manifest, through the Universal Law of Mind, as the very experiences of our life. It addresses the creative nature of *all* thought and the tendency of our individual thoughts and words to take form not only when we are *specifically* praying for a desired result, but also as we think and speak in our daily life.

Ernest Holmes, the Founder of Religious Science, wrote in *The Science of Mind:* "The subjective state of thought is a power always at work; it is the result of the sum total of all beliefs, consciously and unconsciously held."[1] Our beliefs, consciously and unconsciously held, become the thoughts, words, feelings, and actions in our daily life.

Though we may consciously speak words of Truth in our Spiritual Mind Treatments, Affirmative Prayers, and Creative Meditations—acknowledging Spirit as All-in-all, as *always* present and the *only* Creative Power in, through, and *as* ourselves—often between our prayers we think and speak *un*consciously from the habitual patterns of beliefs we have accepted and no longer question as *reality*.

Our accumulated beliefs, and their expression through our thoughts, words, feelings, and actions, do

1. SOM 322.2

1

not always support the words we have spoken in prayer. Instead they reflect a material rather than spiritual basis for our daily living where Truth is not recognized as being constantly present and active as Love *and* Law, and the power of our word to create through the Law is disregarded.

This dualistic way of thinking and speaking tends to nullify our prayers by opposing the very words we *officially* "send forth into the Law," and it has the potential to reinforce as *real* and *unchangeable* the very thing we sought to change, improve, heal, or reveal through prayer.

Therefore, if we want to change our lives for Good, we must become aware of our thoughts and words as we think and speak them, because the space *between* prayers is sacred, too. Whether we are acknowledging and directing It or not, the Presence is *always* present, and the Creative Power within us is *always* at work turning our thoughts into things and our words into the experiences of our life.

How do we live in the *continuous* recognition that God is ever-present *as* ourselves in form and *as* ourselves in function, *always*—and not only when we pray? Or, to put the matter another way: how do we live in the *constant* recognition that we are an individualization of Spirit—the One, All-knowing, All-powerful Creative Consciousness—and that we continuously replicate the unending Creativity of the Macrocosm *through the One Law of Being* in the microcosm of our day-to-day life?

When Paul of the New Testament told his followers to "pray without ceasing,"[2] surely he wasn't suggesting that everyone stay on their knees twenty-four hours a day or walk around Thessalonica with their eyes closed and their fingertips pointing upwards. Instead, he may have been showing us a way to unceasingly live in the conscious recognition of the Presence of Love and the Power of the One Law of Being to act upon our conscious and unconscious thoughts and words.

Ernest Holmes suggested that to pray without ceasing is to *constantly* recognize "our relationship to that Presence in which we live and move and have our being."[3] In the Glossary of *The Science of Mind*, Dr. Holmes defined that Presence: "'The Presence' is God."[4]

A *constant* recognition, according to the dictionary definition of the word *constant*, is a continuously occurring awareness that is "persistent; unchanging in nature, value, or extent; invariable." If we were to pray without ceasing—that is, consider each thought and word as being as potent as a Treatment, Affirmative Prayer, or Creative Meditation—*all* of our thoughts

2. I Thessalonians 5:17 (KJV)
3. SOM 497.1
4. SOM 621, s.v. "Presence"

and words would be unchanging in their spiritual nature, value, and extent, and they would be invariable in their ability to create "heaven on earth."

If our life doesn't resemble the Truth we speak in our prayers, it is likely that *between* our prayers our thoughts vary and change in their perceived nature and value. When we are not specifically praying, our mental perceptions often fluctuate between an awareness of our oneness in the *spiritual* life and a belief in our separateness in a *material* life. Frequently the value we place upon the efficacy of our words spoken in prayer decreases as we look to the outer world, and not to our beliefs, as the source and supply in our life.

We wonder why our Treatments, Affirmative Prayers, and Creative Meditations don't seem to "work," and we frequently blame ourselves for our lack of spiritual conviction when we pray. However, more often than not the problem does not lie in our confidence *when* we pray. In those sacred moments when we turn within, recognize Spirit as the Source and Substance of all, and consciously sense our oneness with It, it is easy to feel assured that we have realized the very essence of Truth. In such an exalted, sacred condition, we are certain that all things are possible, change is inevitable, and healing is guaranteed.

But it is often our lack of certainty and our opposing beliefs *between* our prayers—as we go about what we have determined as the "mundane" business of daily living, which often appears to belie confirmation of Spirit—that affects the efficacy of the words we have spoken in prayer. If we want to *permanently* change our life, it is the consciousness we maintain between our prayers that we need to examine.

How many of us who speak our words regularly or periodically in the form of Treatment, Affirmative Prayer, or Creative Meditation recognize that "the Presence is God" *always*, and in *all* things, and not merely when we recognize It as such? When we open our eyes and look into the world, are we still consciously aware that God is the *only* Presence—that Spirit is not only the Cause (Love) and Creator (Law) of our moment-to-moment life *as it is*, but that Spirit *is* the very shape and form of *all* that we see?

Do we recognize Spirit here and now *on earth?* Or, when we are not praying, do we relegate Spirit to the unseen realm of Cause and think of It as an Energy and Creative Medium *separate* from the material world, awaiting our next prayer or treatment before It manifests according to our official word?

Do we *persistently* unify with Spirit, unshakably convinced of our relationship as Its image and likeness, and do we recognize that we think *into* It and speak *into* It every moment? Do we realize without ceasing that we do not (because it is not possible) live and move and have our being in any other life but the One Manifested Life—and that Life through the Law of Being is constantly creating everything, everywhere, all of the time, including right where we are, through our thoughts and words?

Science has proven through comprehensive studies on the subject that there is power in prayer. Spiritual Mind Treatment, Affirmative Prayer, and Creative Meditation are effective because they clear "the thought of negation, of doubt and fear, and [cause] it to perceive the ever-presence of God."[5] If we return to negative thoughts of doubt and fear after we have prayed, we blind ourselves to the Truth we have spoken within the clarity of our prayers.

There is no doubt or fear in the All-knowing, All-powerful, Ever-present Consciousness of the Divine, with which we unify in prayer, and in Truth there is no other Consciousness—no separate, personal consciousness—between our prayers. However, when we are not praying, our sense of self frequently feels separate, and our mind seems isolated within us rather than connected to the One Infinite Mind. Our oneness with the One becomes a theory rather than a practice, something to talk about rather than *Something* to experience.

If we want consciously to live in the Consciousness

5. SOM 638, s.v. "Treatment"

of our prayers, we must remind ourselves between our prayers that our consciousness is *that* Consciousness. Then we must let the Truth be so alive within us, so real to us, that we cannot be moved from our spiritual conviction of oneness no matter what shape and form of life appears before us. We cannot allow materiality to reign as primary form and substance in our daily experience, and negative thoughts of doubt and fear to be the basis for our personal and world view, and then not expect such patterns of belief to interfere with our perception and experience of Truth.

We need to ask ourselves:

How does my life look, not when I turn away and turn within, but when I face it with my eyes wide open? Am I tempted to view my body and its functions (or dysfunctions), my relationships (and conflicts), my job (or lack of one), and all of the other forms and activities of my personal life and the world as something that is happening to me rather than the manifestation of my thoughts and words? Do I mentally separate who I am in the moment from who I might potentially be one day when my prayers are answered?

We feel wonderful during our Treatments, Affirmative Prayers, and Creative Meditations. Our recognition of Pure Spirit as the Cause and Creator of all that exists, our confidence that the Truth includes ourselves, and our conviction that our thoughts and words are creative, release in us the freedom inherent in our true spiritual nature.

We realize that we and all beings are free from disease, pain, heartache, loneliness, and poverty—for lack and limitation are false in the Truth of Being in which all life moves and has its being. We are grateful for the efficacy of our prayer, we joyfully accept its vision as "complete in Mind and already done," and we let go of those old, limited beliefs as we embrace and embody Truth.

However, when our prayer is complete, only we ourselves can determine if we have truly let go of our false beliefs and accepted a *new reality*, or if we have merely put our old beliefs aside while we've prayed because they did not belong in our Treatment or Creative Meditation. It is important for us to become aware of our thoughts moment-to-moment, and of our words as we speak in the world, for if we are not supporting our prayers, we are most likely defeating them.

It is said that we cannot think of two opposing things at the exact same time. When we are immersed in the conscious awareness of God as All-in-all, our belief in a life apart from God disappears. While we are praying, it is easy for us to suppose that we will not forget the sacred state of oneness that we are experiencing.

But the material word is seductive, and if we do not intentionally maintain our conscious awareness of our immersion in Spirit *and nothing else,* and if we do not continue to realize the efficacy of our thoughts and words between our prayers, then our picture of a life imbued with freedom and fulfillment may revert to material subservience and a world *out there* that we must depend on for our joy and happiness. When Spirit is relegated to the background between prayers and not perceived as the primary picture, it is easy for us to pick up where we left off in attitude and point of view before we prayed and take up the banner of separateness once again.

When we think and speak of our life as separate from God, we cannot recognize the Sacred Life that is ever-present—a Life in which we are always participating whether we are conscious of It or not—and we tend to ignore the power and creativity of our word. There is so much that we say and accept every day about ourselves and others, and the world in general, which runs contrary to what we claim as Truth when we pray.

In our prayers we speak with certainty of our Divine origin and eternal oneness with Spirit. We recognize only the Eternal Moment in which all is new and unfettered by precedent. We affirm that the past is nonexistent and that the future is born of pure Good.

Yet between our prayers we often speak with equal conviction about our personal failures or the inadequacies of others, the pain of the past, the limitations of the present, and our fears of the future. It is as if we draw one picture of our life when we pray and then draw a different picture over it between our prayers. Neither picture is clearly recognizable, but certainly the one that has the thicker lines and deeper impressions will be the most visible.

How many *double impressions* are we making in our life? How often between our prayers do we talk about (in full color and detail!) the very disease whose nonexistence we spoke of in our Treatment? How often do we gossip about and judge harshly the very people we spoke of as being "whole, complete, and perfect" in our prayer? Too often we *scribble over* and blur the vision of the perfection of Life we have seen in our prayers with thoughts and words that consist of thick lines of separateness and deep impressions of doubt and fear.

We cannot achieve moment-to-moment clarity—out of which our highest thoughts and greatest inspirations come forth—as long as we believe that we can have it both ways, i.e., see two pictures at the same time any time we choose. And we cannot perceive the Truth within the Present Moment as long as we continue to insist that two *truths* can go on simultaneously but separately—the perfect realm of Spirit and the imperfect realm of matter.

It is easy to forget, given the seemingly solid divisions of material life, that "the things which are seen came to be from those which are not seen."[6] It is even easier to forget that what is seen *is* Spirit in form and *not* something else, a foreign substance, that has no connection to the purity of God. If we do not intentionally begin each thought with Spirit as the only Cause and Creator, as we do in our prayers, we are likely to arrive at material—and therefore *limited, divisive, destructive, disease-forming, impoverished, and fearful*—conclusions that inadvertently create a life for us that resembles little of the powerful, spiritual Life we speak of in our prayers.

If we desire to *constantly* experience our relationship to Spirit, rather than only *occasionally* in our moments of prayer, and if we desire to live the life of freedom that is innately ours as spiritual beings, then we must choose to live in the moment-to-moment spiritual *context* of Spirit as all. Then we shall be motivated by Love, inspired by Joy, directed by Wisdom, and balanced in Peace.

---

6. Hebrews 11:3 (Lamsa)

Out of this sacred space our thoughts and words will spring forth and our actions will be enlightened by a greater awareness than we could achieve in "ordinary moments." A mind open to the Infinite is inspired in length, depth, and breadth. Its creativity is *not* limited to satisfying its own isolated needs (yet these needs *are* satisfied, for it is written, "Seek first the kingdom of God and his righteousness, and all these things shall be added to you"[7]). It is *not* concerned with getting enough, getting more, getting even. It is *not* concerned with being right, being understood, being in control. It does *not* fear the past, overlook the present, or doubt the future.

When our mind is *constantly* open to Infinite Mind, we are inspired in all our ways, in *and between* our prayers. Our every thought, word, and deed is imbued with Wisdom and Compassion. We perceive the wholeness of all life, including ourselves. We become an emissary of love, an ambassador of peace, a messenger of hope, a purveyor of wisdom, and an instrument of healing—because all life is One.

It is incumbent upon us to view Treatment, Affirmative Prayer, and Creative Meditation not as formal, periodic *spiritual injunctions* for getting what we want or for changing what we don't want, but as a formula for living each moment—because the truth of the matter is that when we are not "officially" using these creative forms of prayer to move our thoughts

7. Matthew 6:33 (Lamsa)

along a specific meditation; when we are not "speaking our word" for a specific purpose; when we are between our specialized prayers: the Creative Power that would and does bring about the manifestation of our prayers is *still* operative.

In other words, the Presence is still present whether we are acknowledging It in prayer or ignoring It as we think and speak in our everyday lives. Universal Creative Energy doesn't turn off or go somewhere else until we are ready to "use" It in our Treatments. It is everywhere all of the time, and It is always active—whether we're ready or not.

How to Use It

As LONG AS both Creator and creation *exist;* as long as the One Being is being *something;* as long as there is existence, actually or potentially: the Creative Medium of Spirit is active. We live and move and have our being within the activity of this Creative Medium, which is the Mental Law of the Universe. As long as we, the image and likeness of Spirit, are consciously *being,* we are being *something*—and we set the Law in motion with our every thought and word.

What we are being depends upon our beliefs, and our beliefs are reflected in our thoughts, words, feelings, and actions. Just as the Word of God is Cause universally, the word of God *as* ourselves causes our individual and collective life experience. It is important for us to remember, though, that no matter what appears to be, and regardless of who appears to be doing it, there is only One Being *being*—everywhere, all of the time—as all that exists.

There is no limitation to the Law of Spirit and the Creative Process universally or individually. Each individual (and collectively, all individuals) reenact the Creative Process in every detail of daily life. Our thoughts and words operate through the One Mental Law, and our experience of Life is limited only by our belief in and acceptance of *What Is* in each moment.

When speaking of the creative nature and power of the word, spoken and unspoken, Ernest Holmes wrote in the chapter "How to Use It," in *The Science of Mind:* "It has been proved that by thinking correctly and by a conscious mental use of the Law of Mind, we can cause It to do definite things for us, through us."[8]

This same chapter discusses one of the basic Principles of mental healing, and in it Dr. Holmes focuses *not* on how we can *use* the Law of Mind per se, but rather on how we can use it *correctly.* There is never an indication or even a suggestion that the *use* of the Law of Mind is voluntary or that It can be used sporadically or periodically. Our use of the Law of Mind is automatic and immutable; we *use* It every time we think.

We are constantly surrounded by and irrevocably immersed in the Law of Mind—the Receptive, Creative Energy and Substance which responds to thought—*all* thought, *all* the time. There is no evading the Law, because, as we have already seen, there is nowhere outside of the Absolute that we could exist. The Law is Infinite and is right where we are, wherever we are. It "flows through us, because It flows through everything, and since we exist, It must be in and through us. This is the crux of the whole matter."[9]

Our choice is not whether to *use* It, but whether to use It *correctly.* If we do not learn to use It *correctly*— i.e., if our moment-to-moment thoughts are not based

8. SOM 52.3
9. SOM 52.2

upon the conviction that "the (only) Presence is God" and that our thoughts and words are creative (and *never* meaningless or inert), there is a good chance that we will create a world of trouble!

We are intrinsically and unavoidably creative. We can't help it. It's just the way we're made: in the image and likeness of God. That is why it is critical for us to live consciously, rather than habitually, and not to allow inner patterns of belief to go unchecked or unchanged.

To use the Law of Mind *correctly*, we must begin by recognizing Its constant Presence and Activity as *our* mind and then ask ourselves: "What am I thinking in *this* moment? What am I *recognizing* as my life right now, and what am I *unifying with* in this experience?"

It is vital for us to be conscious and awake to our every thought, for every thought is a prayer, whether it is officially designated as such or not; and if it is true that "we cannot say that one thought will create while another will not,"[10] then whether or not we are using Treatment, Affirmative Prayer, or Creative Meditation to move our thought, every time we think, our thought moves.

We have all heard the familiar metaphor that *thoughts fall like seeds into the rich soil of Creative Consciousness,* but how often do we realize the consequences of such an activity? How frequently do we consciously consider the fact that our every thought is like a seed and—positive or negative, good seed or

10. SOM 94.1

"bad"—a thought has everything it requires to grow in the garden of our individual and global experience.

If we begin our day speaking our word in prayer, affirming the ever-presence of Spirit in, above, through, and as all life—and acknowledging the Power of our word to affect and change our life through the unceasing activity of the Law of Mind— we cannot afford *not* to support our prayer with joy-filled, life-enriching, spiritually-based thoughts every moment throughout our day.

> *Undoubtedly, each of us is now demonstrating his concept of life, but trained thought is far more powerful than untrained, and the one who gives conscious power to his thought should be more careful what he thinks than the one who does not.*[11]

Thoughts that are inspired by fear—e.g., a belief in an isolated self, a divided world—and all of the thoughts, words, and feelings of aggression, defensiveness, distrust, and prejudice these beliefs engender are just as creatively potent in our daily life as the words we speak about Love, Peace, and Power in our prayers.

If we want to truly live the life we speak of in our prayers, we must continuously remind ourselves that every thought is generative regardless if we have consciously and specifically "planted" it using prayer or not. As anyone who has planted a garden knows, some things grow through conscious intention and action.

11. SOM 47.2

But others sprout from seeds invisibly blown in by the wind or from "opportunistic" seeds buried in the soil awaiting the perfect environment for growth.

A mind that has given recognition to Spirit for a few moments a day but that is focused on the world at large as something separate from Spirit the rest of the day is, through the Universal Law of Mind, susceptible to the seeds (and weeds) of the "collective unconscious" and is likely to accept as *true*, jump on the bandwagon *for*, and fight against as *real* the myriad manifestations of separation and alienation.

We cannot serve God *and* mammon. It is our *spiritual fluctuations* that keep us from experiencing both unshakable faith in, and undeniable embodiment of, the Truth we speak in our prayers. Such vacillation prevents true change and permanent transformation in our life.

It is as if between our prayers we "unravel" the very vision of Truth we have seen in our Treatments and Creative Meditations. It is much like the elderly woman who could be seen busily knitting each day but who never produced a finished garment. She loved to knit, and her *knit* stitch was beautiful, but she was too embarrassed to admit that she'd never learned the crucial *purl* stitch necessary to turn a ball of yarn into something practical. So each night she unraveled her work, and in the morning she began knitting all over again. In this way her work was always *in progress* and she never had to consider what a *completed* piece might look like.

Unless we learn to support our prayers with our daily thoughts and words rather than unraveling them with opposing thoughts of doubt and fear, and unless we make our prayers practical in, and applicable to, our moment-to-moment activities, we shall not experience ourselves as whole, a *complete* expression of Spirit, something beautiful, fulfilled and lacking nothing. Instead we shall continue to feel incomplete, a *work in progress* that is neither completely material nor wholly spiritual.

To use the Law of Mind *correctly* is to think into It *only* that which we wish to experience in form. There is still power in the word when it is not spoken as a prayer, and our words, both *silent* and *oral,* are equally creative. We must not allow ourselves to forget that we exist within the Responsive, Creative Substance of the Divine—and that there is no way out of the Fertile Soil of Subjectivity. The procreant nature of the Creative Medium in which all form takes shape cannot be stripped of Its Potent Originative Power through our ignorance, neglect, or misuse of It.

Whenever we think, we think into It; whenever we speak, we speak into It; wherever we go, we cannot go away from It. There is no place outside of the Boundless, no existence beyond the Unlimited, no form, formula, or formulator separate from the All-

Inclusive. We cannot circumvent the Law of Cause and Effect simply by ignoring the sacred fact that we're in *It*, and It is in *us*, moment to moment, day and night, good times and bad, for better or worse.

We cannot bypass the Law through blindness or negligence, or by making excuses for how we are thinking or what we are saying when we're not praying. It matters not that we've been too preoccupied with our worldly obligations or seduced by our material possessions to think "spiritually." In every moment, Spirit moves upon the waters of our existence—whether we're thinking *spiritually or materially*—turning thoughts into things, words into forms, and the sum total of our *inner world* of beliefs into the experiences of our *outer world*.

Rather than our prayers being mere spiritual oases where we retreat from the bad and the ugly of daily living and seek to change it, Treatment, Affirmative Prayer, or Creative Meditation can serve as a permanent template for our moment-to-moment perception of *What Is* in the face of what may *appear to be*. The act of perceiving *What Is* is by no means passive. It is an active, intentional opening within ourselves that enables us to recognize Spirit as the only Presence in every moment.

From this higher, broader perception we are more capable of giving the Creative Power of Spirit more meaningful directive expression through our thoughts, words, and actions. The activity of perceiving *What Is* is an exercise in spiritual awareness that allows us to recognize the Presence of Peace in the midst of violence, war, and chaos; the Presence of Love in the midst of abuse and abandonment; the Presence of Joy in the midst of sorrow and pain; and the Presence of Abundance in the midst of limitation and poverty.

The Truth is revealed to the mind set upon Infinite Spirit, and Its revelation resolves and dissolves any appearance of opposition. It is out of this vigilant practice of spiritual perception that inspiration comes forth in the form of thoughts, words, and actions. It provides a clarity of perception that allows us to experience the Grace and Glory of Life here and now, and not just now and then.

Spiritual Mind Treatment, Affirmative Prayer, and Creative Meditation give us the *only* place to start if we want to turn our world *inside out* so that Spirit—all that is good, real, and beautiful—is revealed as the only Life that *Is*. We can use these creative forms of prayer as a formula for using the Law *correctly* and living our life on a spiritual basis, not only when we pray, but every moment in between.

Spiritual Mind Treatment: A Formula for Thought

THE FOLLOWING SECTIONS are based upon the five steps of Spiritual Mind Treatment:

1. RECOGNITION
2. UNIFICATION
3. REALIZATION
4. THANKSGIVING
5. RELEASE

As mentioned earlier, Creative Meditations and Affirmative Prayers may not include these five steps specifically, but they are generally based upon the same Principles:

Spirit is All-in-all.

Every individual maintains an irrevocable, unchanging oneness with Spirit.

All life is perfect as it proceeds from Spirit and is revealed through the word, spoken and unspoken, which is acted upon by Universal Law.

An attitude of gratitude reflects an embodiment of Wholeness.

The Truth is revealed as opposition to It is released.

A Note about Praying for Others: Our consciousness, as an individualization of the One Consciousness, includes all life forms. Because we are one with the One, we are inseparably one with all. The Truth is not exclusive, and therefore there has been no distinction made here between our perceiving the perfection about *ourselves* and our perceiving it about *another,* in or between our prayers.

"In whose mind is [the practitioner] to become conscious of perfection? In the only person's mind he can ever be conscious of anything, in his own mind."[12] To think of ourselves or speak of ourselves as praying for "another" is a subtle form of dualism, for Consciousness is One. The Truth we perceive about anyone or anything reveals Itself within *our* consciousness, but because Consciousness is One and affects the totality of our awareness of all things, we become more aware of the Truth of *What Is* in everyone we see and in all of our experiences.

12. SOM 409.1

The First Step

For I am God, and there is none else.[13]

All there really is, is God![14]

---

13. Isaiah 45:22
14. SOM 188.3

Recognition

A SPIRITUAL MIND TREATMENT begins at the *beginning*—by starting with *Nothing at all.*

The Infinite of Itself is Formless but within It are contained all the forms which give expression to Its consciousness. Spirit is the Limitless within which is all space. Spirit is Timeless, within which is all time.[15]

Spiritual Mind Treatment begins, then, with the **Recognition** of Pure, Formless Life within the Unlimited, Eternal Moment (*every* moment is *that* moment). There is no life in the universe that Spirit is not *already* being. There is no time when It is not present. There is no shape or form that does not begin within It. There is nothing that moves or exists without It.

This Recognition is not a recognition of some Thing separate from ourselves or a petition to a far-off God who may or may not grant our request. Spiritual Mind Treatment is not a supplication to an external, authoritarian Deity who is moved by the anguished, beseeching prayers of His children or by their "good deeds." It is not a prayer *to* anything at all.

Rather, the first step is a recognition of One Life, Spirit as All-in-all, Creator *and* Creation.

---

15. SOM 66.5

ᐘ It is a recognition of the Creative Principle *behind* the eternal process of creation even as It is *within* it.

ᐘ It is a recognition of the Divine Intelligence that moves like a kaleidoscope with every thought, idea, and notion and yet is beyond all thoughts, ideas, and notions.

ᐘ It is a recognition of the Pure Substance and Undifferentiated Being that causes all to be.

ᐘ It is a recognition of the Eternal Life Force continually creating, moment-to-moment.

ᐘ It is a recognition of the Presence that is everywhere *always*.

Such a recognition discounts the existence of a tear in the Fabric of the Soul, a rip in the Web of Life, an otherness in the Great Nest of Being. Because there can be no boundary to the Limitless, no end to the Timeless, and no gap in the Wholeness through which any part of Creation could fall to begin a separate life away from Spirit, this first step of Recognition covers all the bases. It's *All* and *Nothing!*

NAMING THE NAMELESS

Though ancient wisdom and modern intelligence acknowledge that the Indescribable cannot be described, nonetheless in this first step, as we recognize the Allness of Spirit, we often attribute to It our highest abstract notions of Good. "We describe It as God,

Spirit, Reality, Truth—Absolute Intelligence,"[16] Love, Wisdom, Joy, Peace, Power. Spiritual Mind Treatment begins with the recognition of these qualities as the only Presence and the only Reality.

A consciousness immersed in Boundless, Infinite Spirit cannot be aware of anything else. There can be no "us *and* them" nor can there be a "self *and* God." In the Allness of Spirit there is ultimately only One Being—*being*.

This first step is an abstract state of awareness. It is an illumined perspicacity which occurs before our individual concept of a personal self, before we speak the words "I AM." It is the recognition of Conscious Intelligence, Directive Power, Unlimited Wisdom, Pure Creative Energy, and Universal Potential awaiting our word. "It is ready to become molded into any or all forms. It is unexpressed Power, Substance and Creativeness. It is unexpressed Mind. It waits to be called into form or expression."[17]

Who does the calling? As far as our experience of life goes, *we* do—with the beliefs we hold, consciously and unconsciously, and with every thought that we think and every word that we speak.

16. SOM 66.2
17. SOM 392.2

Step 2

"The Inside Step"

I and my Father are one.[18]

To each of us, individually, God or Spirit is the
Supreme Personality of the Universe—
the Supreme Personality
of that which we, ourselves, are.[19]

18. John 10:30 (KJV)
19. SOM 330.5

Unification

THE SECOND STEP of Spiritual Mind Treatment, **Unification**, is a conscious declaration of unity with Spirit. We affirm that there can be *no* separation between ourselves and God because right where we are, God Is. We understand that we are not dual in nature—not shadow *and* light, material *and* spiritual, being *and* becoming—but singular, one with *the One*. We have no doubt of this, because we have recognized in our first step of Treatment that God is All-in-all. Therefore there cannot be God *and* anything else, including ourselves.

In our deepest meditations, we may experience moments of "nonthought," a state of consciousness beyond space, time, and form. But it is important for us to remember that the Unformed Creative Energy that is poised in these moments of nonthought is stimulated into action with our next thought or mental image.

In our prayers, we consciously declare "I am one with Spirit," and we attribute all that we are to the Spirit of our origin. However, each of us is also declaring "I am" with our every thought, word, and action *between* our prayers. *All* thought is given "Creative Attention," and therefore it is vital for us to become conscious of what we are attributing to ourselves and to life between our prayers. What we declare about ourselves every moment of every day, and what we affirm as the condition of the world, is given the form of our belief.

We are made *in* and *of* Spirit, Divine Consciousness, and we are imbued with the nature of the Divine. We are self-conscious, creative beings—and just as Spirit through Self-Contemplation endlessly originates all life through the Law of Mind, we continuously recreate in *image and likeness* what we believe about ourselves and life.

To think of ourselves as a *channel* through which Spirit speaks or heals is to deny the allness of Spirit by perceiving ourselves as "something else," a conduit *for* the Divine rather than a being *of* the Divine.

Spirit speaks *as* us, because the mind with which we think *is* God, whether we are looking "through a glass darkly" or seeing "face to face." The unexpressed Mind waiting to be called into form and expression is Spirit individualized within each of us. Our every thought is the Word of God made flesh, reflecting the Original command, "Let there be life."

There Is a Perfect Union

"In Treatment there should always be a recognition of the absolute unity of God and man."[20] Yet we should also recognize that even though we are consciously unifying with God, there has never been a time when we were *not* unified with God. We are always *in* God,

20. SOM 331.2

and God *is* always *us.*

In the stillness of a consciousness that recognizes this Truth of Being, a consciousness that recognizes no separate agenda, a consciousness that has surrendered self-indulgent estimates of right and wrong, Truth, unfettered by opposites and opposition, inspires thought and word but never denies individuality.

Whatever thoughts, concepts, and notions come forth from that pure state of awareness arrive *trailing clouds of glory.* Whatever ideas are born of this clarity of being are shaped and formed by Divine Wisdom and express the perfection, grace, beauty, harmony, and peace that spring forth from that Presence.

What absolute clarity and conviction such a conscious unification brings to our sense of being—for in our Treatments we dwell in that perfect state of awareness of what we are *already!* And from this high awareness, from this elevated sense of oneness with the Power of the Universe, we speak knowing that nothing can hinder the power of the word. "It is here that the mentality performs seeming miracles, *because there is nothing to hinder the Whole from coming through.*"[21]

CORRECTING A "MISUNDERSTANDING"

Our conscious unification with the Power and Presence of God is a sacred condition of spiritual understanding—an irrefutable knowledge of ourselves as spiritual beings, whole, complete, and perfect just as

21. SOM 358.3

we are. Keeping this in mind, we could then say that any other concept of ourselves, any other perception of being, that precluded such a sacred condition of understanding would be a *mis*understanding, an error in perception, a lack of true knowing.

No doubt we all have experienced the tangled web of unfortunate and painful circumstances that can follow a misunderstanding. When we misinterpret someone's intention towards us, we make choices based upon our error. If we believe that a person doesn't like us because we have misunderstood something that was said or done, we may invent reasons to dislike that person and to exclude him or her from participating in our life. We might share our feelings with a third party and in the process, alienate that person from the one we've misunderstood.

The chain of events that result from a misunderstanding can often be disastrous. We experience the alienation and separation built upon our negative perceptions—and all of the life-depleting emotions attendant on them—and miss out altogether on the potential joy inherent in the "true" intentions that we have *mis*understood.

When we do not *consciously* dwell in that sacred space of spiritual understanding in which we know that we are one with *that* Presence, always, we miss out on the joy inherent in God's intention for us, i.e., the Kingdom of Heaven. We do not feel the empowerment that comes from a *constant* awareness of what we are *already* and, rather than experiencing the ceaseless Good that "God intended," our days often unfold in a chain of unfortunate and painful experiences.

Without our *conscious* unification with Universal Creative Power—which is *always* giving form to our *every* thought and word through our unbroken, irrevocable intercourse with It—we do not experience the freedom of knowing the Power behind (and in) our word moment-to-moment. Our time is often spent in the *dis*empowering and futile search for fulfillment in a world of material things that we perceive as separate from ourselves.

We struggle to accumulate wealth, acquire health, find love, achieve peace, and manufacture joy out of *material substance*—and seek *spiritual substance* and a conscious unification with Spirit only when we run into the roadblocks, setbacks, pain, and suffering we've created through our daily misunderstanding of who we are *already*. Then we pray for the revelation of Spirit in our life, when in actuality the One Life has been present *as* our life all along.

WHAT DO YOU HAVE TO SAY FOR YOURSELF?

How we think *of* ourselves and the way we speak *to* ourselves affects every area of our life. Our self-talk is so habitual and familiar that we seldom realize what we are saying until the subjective images we've planted "spring up" as our life experience. Then we are motivated to stop and consider that perhaps our unconscious, repetitive, and deep-seated thinking—as well as our self-concept in general between our prayers—may have inadvertently taken us somewhere we didn't want to be.

It is important for us to become aware of what we are thinking *about* ourselves when we are not praying *for* ourselves. For instance, how do we think of our "personality" in the space between our prayers? Are we still convinced that "God, or Spirit, is Supreme, Infinite, Limitless Personality,"[22] and that we are "One with the personality of God,"[23] or do we vary our self-concepts by contrasting and comparing ourselves to others? Are we boastful or shy? Do feel superior or inferior to others? Do we circumscribe our personalities by limiting ourselves to an astrological sign, inherited mannerisms, or unchangeable traumatic influences? Do we tell the same old stories that seem to give color to our personality and make us special, and use our stories as excuses for our *mis*behavior?

Many therapists believe that we should, even *must*, tell our stories of pain and injury, because suppressed traumas often appear as physical and emotional conditions. This may be "factual," but the benefit of bringing the past into the present is so that we can heal it by letting go of old perspectives in exchange for new ones. If we continue to regurgitate the past because it

22. SOM 362.3
23. SOM 296.4

seems more interesting than the present, we not only recreate old problems and validate poor self-images, but in the process we tend to reinforce our misunderstanding that we are ever separate from Spirit.

In Spiritual Mind Treatment our thought is guided step-by-step into a complete conscious immersion in Spirit, but we cannot sustain such an awareness if, between our prayers, we do not support the concept of spiritual oneness through the same step-by-step process. We must be willing to release repetitive thoughts of who we believe that we *have been* in the world—no matter how benign or amusing our images of a separate self might be—in order to embrace a process of thinking and speaking that reflects a *constant* recognition of the spiritual being that we *already* are.

We do not need to collect painful souvenirs along life's path to show people where we've been or to convince ourselves that we are uniquely individual. We are *original* in Spirit, issuing forth from *the heavens,* a one-of-a-kind expression of the One Expresser.

As we consciously unify with Spirit, we realize that the Kingdom of Heaven is here and now, and that through the Power of our word—spoken and unspoken—within the Sacred Continuum of existence, we can experience Heaven on earth.

Step 3

"The Step Out"

And whatever you ask in my name,
I will do it for you, so that the Father
may be glorified through his Son.[24]

The man who dares to fling his thought out
into Universal Intelligence,
with the assurance of one who realizes
his divine nature and its relation to the Universe—and
dares to claim all there is—will find an ever-creative
good at hand to aid him.[25]

24. John 14:13
25. SOM 142.3

Realization

IN THE THIRD STEP of Spiritual Mind Treatment, **Realization,** we are convinced that "what we speak is the law unto the thing spoken," because Spirit is All, and we are one with Spirit and the Inexhaustible Creative Power of the Universe. In Realization we are certain of the unlimited nature of our self-expression, and we do not doubt the power of our word, spoken into Law, to manifest all that we have articulated.

We realize that there is no time required for the manifestation of our word, for Spirit dwells in the Eternal Moment, and *that* moment is "here and now," right where we are as we speak our word. We realize that we are not *becoming* whole, but that we *already are*—for what is True in Mind *already Is.* We are convinced that there can be no disease, dysfunction, or disharmony within us, or in any part of life, for we perceive the Truth as It *Is,* perfect already. We realize Spirit is expressing as our body, our relationships, our finances, and all of our activities, and we realize that this is the Truth for all beings.

In our Treatments old patterns of self-identification disappear in the all-enveloping recognition of God as all and our uncompromising unity with It. We perceive that all that we are and express in form and action is derived solely from Spirit, and we realize that all that issues forth as the result of our Treatment is made flesh through our unceasing and invariable sacred relationship to the Soul and Substance of the Universe. Within our Treatments we realize that nothing is impossible to Spirit expressing in, through, and as ourselves.

SUSTAINING OUR CONSCIOUS CONNECTION BETWEEN PRAYERS

Our conscious awareness of our connection to the Creative Power of the Universe has the potential to transform our lives and change the world of appearances; and it would, *if* our conscious awareness of spiritual being were sustained between our prayers. But too often we turn away from the realization of wholeness that we have achieved in our Treatments and return to a perception of a world separate from us, divided against itself, and disconnected from Spirit.

How shall we experience the depth and breadth of *What Is* in each moment if we don't give Truth a chance to be seen or heard?

> *The Spirit is not something apart from matter so-called, but is something working through matter; the potential possibility of what we call the highest and the lowest is inherent in everything. They are not different things.*[26]

The "potential possibility" of the highest is present in every moment and only awaits our thought and

26. SOM 124.1

word, our belief and calling, to become visible to us. The God that would make "all things new" is limited by our memory, presumptions, and hardened beliefs. How can the Truth of *What Is* reveal Itself when we are constantly remembering *what was,* condemning *what is,* and determining *what ought to be?*

How can we participate in the continuous and profound revelation of Spirit within, through, above, beneath, and *as* the very space we're in if we return from our prayerful realizations of spiritual *being* to a perceived world of spiritual *becoming*—where we excuse our human foibles, accuse our human adversaries, and achieve finite and temporary human solutions to the manifestations of divisiveness and disunity that our fluctuations in spiritual realization have created? How will we experience the Truth of *What Is* if we allow the Light of Truth—which floods every moment with Its Glory—only to filter through our dense concepts of a life separate from Spirit when we are not praying?

If we continue to believe that our true spiritual state is somewhere down the road and that it can only be glimpsed momentarily in our Treatments, and if we cling to the idea that "Shangri-la" requires an endless trek, when shall we get there? New Thinkers are those who are open to New Thought—to a *new influx of Spirit* and the *possibilities* inherent in each moment. "Life reveals itself to whoever is receptive to it."[27]

27. SOM 32:2

When we "let that mind be" in us "that was also in Christ Jesus," we realize that there is no *spiritual distance* to travel, no *becoming* to do, no *healing* required. Our individual life and the world around us cease to appear to be a "fixer-upper," a place where Good is only partially expressed and dimly seen. And, when we realize that *our* mind *is* the same mind that was in Christ Jesus, we know beyond a shadow of a doubt that our *every* thought and word is empowered by the Creative Power of the Universe and that there is nothing to oppose the Good that we are and the Good that Life *Is*.

Perpetual Perfection

When we realize that there is no space where God is not, we move through our days confident that we shall meet *only* God in one another, *as* one another. We respect and trust each other because we hear the Voice of Love in our conversations. Loneliness disappears in our sustained knowledge that Love is expressing everywhere *always,* including right where we are.

We maintain poise and calm wherever we are because we realize that Peace *Is* at our center, and at the center of all that exists, because Its center is everywhere. We do not *seek* It in the world through manipulation and control or through acquiescence and submission, but rather we *see* It in the world, because we realize that Peace is the natural expression of the Divine Nature, which is always Present.

We realize that we cannot be deficient in any way, because we know that Spirit is Substance and Supply. We "dare to claim all there is" by expressing all that we are, fully confident that "an ever-creative good is at hand" to give form to our every thought and word. We realize that we cannot be *without,* because we are forever *within,* Boundless Good. We live unfettered and free in the understanding that we can never be bound by necessity.

When we perceive every moment as Sacred Space and think into It only that which we wish to experience, we have a greater sense of well-being. We see the Perfection of God reflected in the cell, fiber, and tissue of *every* body. We feel the Energy of the Universe as the very Substance of our being, and we experience uninterrupted health, energy, and vitality. We feel continuously renewed, because we realize that in each moment we are *re*formed by Eternal Substance. We are not concerned about disease, contagion, heredity, aging, and dying, because we realize that we are born of God and live and move and have our being *always* in Ageless, Changeless, Eternal Spirit.

When we affirm the Truth of being moment-to-moment between our prayers, we naturally vibrate to that which is Real, Good, and True. Our search is over, and our journey is without distance as we unfold with a grateful heart within the Sacred Continuum of Beauty, Grace, and Love—our Originative Cause.

Step 4

"THE DANCE STEP"

*I will praise the name of God with a song, and
will magnify him with thanksgiving.*[28]

*I give thanks that I am Divine and that I know my
Divinity. A sacred refuge is this inner place
where my thought contacts and consciously
becomes one with the Indwelling Almighty.*[29]

28. Psalms 69:30
29. SOM 251.2

Thanksgiving

THE FOURTH STEP of Spiritual Mind Treatment is **Thanksgiving**. It would seem an easy step, for we are all familiar with feelings of gratitude. This *simple* step of joyous thanksgiving and deep appreciation is vital to our Treatment, however, because it affirms our conscious acceptance of the Reality of our spoken word. We are blissfully one with the very image we have spoken into Law—we see it, feel it, and understand its presence as a *tangible* thing within us.

"There must be an appreciation of what the image means, before the image can reflect itself."[30] The sincerity of our feelings of thanksgiving expresses the depth of our belief in the Power of our word, as well as our embodiment (or acceptance as a part of ourselves) of the very thing about which we have prayed. Thanksgiving reflects the realization of our fulfilled spiritual state of being, our *true being*, in which need is dissolved because Fulfillment *already Is*.

When something is right where we are, we don't speak of it as if it were missing. Yet between our prayers we often speak as if we've only window-shopped in our Treatments. We've seen what we want—we're certain that it is *there* in Mind—but we don't *have* it yet.

When we separate Spirit from the moment-to-moment material life we live—and view the images in

30. SOM 176.1

Mind that we have seen in prayer (and affirmed as already Present) as different from what we see with our eyes—we do not feel the fulfillment of answered prayer. Instead we await gratification and postpone true thanksgiving until we have "the goods in hand."

How can we live our days "praising the name of God with a song" of Joy for all that we *already are* and "magnifying him with thanksgiving" when we speak as if that which is *Reality in Mind* hasn't reached the same status of reality in our life?

When we do not truly realize that that which we have declared as *Everywhere Present* is already "with us," we continue to bemoan our meager financial situation, deteriorating physical condition, inharmonious relationships, and lack of fulfillment—rather than celebrating the Creativity of the Spirit and the Power of our word.

"An attitude of gratitude is most salutary, and bespeaks the realization that we are *now* in heaven."[31] Our attitude of gratitude in Treatment proclaims our acceptance of spiritual reality *now*. Thanksgiving is an expression of Spirit Itself, for the gratitude we but faintly feel has its origin and magnitude within Spirit. A heart filled with gratitude is truly at one with the heart of God and bespeaks the recognition of God's intention within creation.

31. SOM 497.2

There Is No End to New Ideas

Between our prayers the world often appears to be far less than the *ideal* we have recognized in our Treatment. It seems overcrowded with meaningless forms and cluttered with the trivial "stuff" of *human* creation. There are thousands of new products offered on the market daily that promise us instant gratification. The human race has created a throwaway society where the "revolutionary" becomes obsolete overnight.

As creative beings dwelling eternally within Unlimited Mind and Boundless Imagination, there is no end to the *new* ideas available to us or to what we are able to manifest in the physical world for our entertainment and comfort. However, when we look to the world for fulfillment, we frequently find that once we've obtained the object we desired, we experience dissatisfaction and boredom rather than sufficiency and joy.

Our Lack Is Not in Things

As human beings, we don't lack *for* things. We lack an *appreciation of* things. For instance, how often do we notice, much less appreciate, the *natural* beauty that is there to be seen in our daily life—a bird singing high atop a telephone pole, a flower growing through the crack in a concrete sidewalk, or the leaves of a tree glistening in the sunlight as we sit in the gridlock of an overcrowded freeway?

In every moment of every day the Good, True, and Beautiful is Present, but we are looking elsewhere—we are looking *for* something we don't have rather than appreciating *What Is*. Rather than taking Life in, we take It for granted and save our gratitude for those occasions when we *finally* get something we wanted.

In our futile search for joy in the world, we have managed to denigrate the very creation we claim to value—we have polluted the oceans, rivers, mountains, meadows, and air of our planet. We stuff yesterday's "hottest new sensations" into our majestic mountains or pile them up in dumps until they become mountains of their own.

If we do not appreciate what we have already, we will not appreciate what we've yet to get. Appreciation is a state of being, a condition of the heart, an "attitude of gratitude." When we are *full* of appreciation, we are fulfilled, and our life is Abundant. We see the miracle in a grain of sand or a blade of grass, and we understand that "the least of these" is Spirit in magnificent form. We appreciate one another, as much for our diversity of form as we do for our similarity in Spirit. We bring our attitude of gratitude to our job, rather than waiting to squeeze out a few moments of satisfaction after hours. Our days are not motivated by what we want to get, but rather they are inspired by all that *Is already*.

THANKSGIVING IS NOT GRATITUDE "TO" GOD

It is easy for us to inadvertently separate ourselves in our mind from the God of creation—and therefore mentally separate ourselves from the sacred disposition behind the life forms we see—when we interpret the Thanksgiving step of Treatment as our being grateful *to* God.

In the first three steps of Treatment, we have recognized God as All, understood ourselves to be one with God, and then realized God as Creator *and* creation; the Cause *and* the effect; the Actor *and* the action. Then we get to the fourth step, Thanksgiving, and rather than continuing to affirm God *only,* God *as* ourselves rather than God *and* ourselves, our Treatment sometimes turns into the traditional prayer of one who believes that he or she is praying *to* God. When we exit our Treatment with this subtle separation in consciousness, it can reestablish the illusion of Spirit *and* the material world as two separate things.

The Thanksgiving step of Treatment is not a *stepping out from* Spirit and *looking back* to say "thank you"; rather it is an expression of Spirit Itself—the unchallenged freedom of Creative Power knowing Itself as All; the unequivocal Joy of Boundless Substance stimulated into unopposed action; the consummate ecstasy of Unimpeded Self-expression issuing forth Its Glory.

"*The faith of God* is very different from *a faith in God.* The faith of God IS God."[32] When we con-

32. SOM 317.3

sciously live in the Sacred Space of Spirit every moment, we have the faith *of* God, for we recognize One Mind only, and we know ourselves to be "a center in the Divine Mind, a point of God-conscious life, truth and action."[33] We experience the unchallenged freedom, unequivocal joy, and consummate ecstasy of one who knows no limit to creativity.

Our thoughts and words no longer fluctuate between identifying with an isolated self-image *and* an individualization of the Divine, and there is no time or effort in the manifestations of Good that we experience. Our days are filled with the joy of *What Is,* in, through, around, and *as* ourselves—and we "magnify" the Truth in all that we do, giving thanks for the word, straight from the heavens, made flesh in all the earth.

33. SOM 56.4

The Final Step

*And no man drinks old wine and immediately wants
new wine; for he says, The old is delicious.*[34]

*It is not easy to release our troubles; we are prone
to linger with them.*[35]

34. Luke 5:39 (Lamsa)
35. SOM 501.4

Release

THE FIFTH AND FINAL STEP in Spiritual Mind Treatment is **Release**. Without this step, we are back where we started from, for our Treatment cannot "take off" to soar in the Unlimited Creativity of our Being while it is weighted down by the limitations of our old, repetitive thoughts, the persistence of our set ideas, and our resistance to change.

If we want to experience *a new influx of Spirit* we must let go of the lesser for the greater, the old for the new, the false for the true, and the relative for the Absolute. Otherwise today looks like yesterday and promises to repeat itself tomorrow.

> *The relative is the Absolute at the level of the relative, and all we mean by the relative is that there is that which has a relationship to something greater than itself. . . . There is not God and something else, but only God in all things. . . . If you wish to see whether or not you are "entering the Absolute," ask yourself, "In my thinking does the answer to this problem depend upon anything past, present or future?" If it does, your treatment stops at that degree of relativity which automatically makes the manifestation contingent upon the decisions already made. . . .[36]*

36. Ernest Homes, *Seminar Lectures*, p. 77.

Thus the full magnitude of our Treatment will either flow unimpeded into our life or else be blocked by the unreleased conditions we have placed upon our relationship to the Absolute.

GOD ANSWERS THROUGH US

The words "I let go and let God" that are often used in the Release step of Spiritual Mind Treatment do not preclude our participation in the *process* of the manifestation of our prayerful words. It is absolutely necessary for us to consciously and actively release the erroneous ideas that we have held which have created the condition for which we are treating. We cannot assume that God can answer prayer *for* us without answering it *through* us.

All healing comes through our conscious awareness, acceptance, and embodiment of Truth as *all*. "God cannot give us anything unless we are in a mental condition to receive the gift. The Law cannot do anything *for* us unless It does it *through* us."[37] We cannot expect to eliminate a *condition* in our life through Spiritual Mind Treatment without eliminating the mental *cause*. And we cannot change our life without changing our thinking, in *and out* of our prayers.

We shall not experience the permanent financial freedom that we declare in Treatment if, between our prayers, we do not release thoughts of lack and poverty. We cannot experience the continuous, uninterrupted

37. SOM 470.1

health that we affirm in Treatment if we do not release harmful, life-depleting thoughts. We cannot continuously experience the harmony in our relationships that we claim in Treatment if we do not release thoughts of anger, distrust, and separation from others.

It is important for us to remember that Release is not our "letting go" *to* God, but rather our letting go *of* old, limited thinking, our releasing any belief in our separation from Spirit, and our letting the Truth appear to our conscious awareness.

God *does* in every moment according to our beliefs, whether we consciously *let* God or not. "One of the most important things for us to remember is that we are always causing something to be created for us."[38] Whether we are thinking small or thinking big, we are *always* thinking into Divine Creative Substance, which gives form to our thoughts.

LETTING GO OF THE LESSER FOR THE GREATER

Our letting go of the meager and recognizing the Almighty *lets* the Truth appear to our consciousness, for what we *see* is what we *get*. As we let go of separation, Love appears; as we let go of disharmony, Peace appears; as we let go of need, Abundant Good appears; as we let go of imperfection, Wholeness appears; and, as we let go of ignorance, Wisdom appears.

When we "let God" be *What Is* in our day-to-day life through our *constant* recognition of *that* Presence

38. SOM 194.5

in which we live and move and have our being—from first step to last, beginning to end, and every Sacred moment in between—we will be *living* rather than merely *doing* our Spiritual Mind Treatments. And, in our moment-to-moment recognition of God as All-in-all, we will experience an *unceasing* "inner realization of the Presence of Perfection within and around about" and we shall hear the Voice of God proclaiming: "I am that which thou art; thou art that which I am."

Consciously Living from Spirit Every Moment

Unconditional Love

THE LOVE WE RECOGNIZE in the first of step of Spiritual Mind Treatment is the only Love that *Is*. It is the Love that is *being* love, always, without qualification or condition. It is a Love that cannot become anything else, because there is nothing else for It to be. It is the Love that has no limitation or opposition; a Love beyond reason and supposition.

"God is Love" has been written in various ways in the scriptures of all religions and spoken from the lips of seers and mystics throughout the ages. It is the Sacred Continuum of Unconditional Love in which we live and move and have our being.

The Love we recognize in Treatment is not the usual love that we so often feel in our day-to-day lives, for frequently our human expressions of love are conditional and temporal. Love swells up within us—capable in its Boundless, Unconditional Nature of embracing the world and everything in it—but our expression of It is often constricted by our fears and limited by our stipulations and assumptions. Rather than recognizing Love as Present as ourselves, we treat It as if It were a variable commodity. We *give* love, *receive* love, *withhold* love, and *lose* love—because we forget that Love is All there *Is,* and that Love is what we *are*.

When we do not know ourselves as Love, our

expressions of love fluctuate. We perceive love as a *choice,* as something that we can choose to give to those who deserve it and to withhold from those who don't. But Love is not a choice; Love is a state of being. Love is what we are, moment-to-moment. We can deny this Truth of our being, but It is still there, closer than our next breath, composing our very existence. We can say "I do not love," but a more accurate statement might be, "I am not experiencing the Love that I am."

The Bible tells us "There is no fear in love; but perfect love casts out fear, because fear is tormenting."[39] Unconditional Love is free from fear, because It has nothing to lose. It is *Love no matter what.* When we forget that Love is always present, we think of It as transitory—here one minute, gone the next. We fall *in* Love as if It were a pleasant pool of bliss and then worry that It might evaporate. We fall *out* of Love as if It were not *everywhere* and then blame ourselves or another for exiling us from It.

The fearful conditions we place on our expressions of Love create torment. Our fear that Love is not all there *Is,* all the time, can turn even our best efforts to love into anxiety, suffocation, jealousy, domination, and manipulation. We say: "I will love you *when . . .*" and "I won't love you *if. . . .*" Imperfect love compels us to try to force the *when* of love by placing demands upon, or accepting the demands of, the object of our

39. I John 4:18 (Lamsa)

affection. Fearful love motivates us to try to prevent the *ifs* of love through attempts to control the outcome of our loving. When we believe that we can *make* love happen and then *prevent* it from leaving, we live in torment.

Perfect Love casts out fear because Perfect Love just *Is*. It is devoid of *when* because It is constant and unchanging. It is free of *ifs* because It is unconditional. We live and move and have our being in Perfect Love in which there is no fear.

We often claim our relationship to Unconditional Love in our Treatments only to go about our day choosing *who* we will love, *when* we will love—or *if* we will love at all! We decide who is worthy of love, and in the process often determine that we, ourselves, are unlovable. "For with the measure that you measure, it will be measured to you."[40] When we believe that Love is something that we can withhold or give according to our assessments of merit, we can usually find plenty of reasons not to love ourselves.

Love cannot disappear between our Treatments. It comprises the Universe. Love is always right where we are, for Love is *What Is*—Perfect, Fearless, and Unconditional. If we are not experiencing and expressing Love in every moment, it is not because Love is not Present. We are born of Unconditional Love, the only Creative Impetus. Love is *What Is* everywhere, all of the time, and Love is what we *are*.

40. Luke 6:38 (Lamsa)

In the hush of Pure Silence that dissolves pain from the past, quiets fears of the future, and nullifies judgment and opinion, Unconditional Love appears—the Voice of God speaking words of Love; the Universal Ear hearing sounds of Love; the Vision of Spirit seeing forms of Love; the Movement of Life expressing Love. For Unconditional Love is What Is—*and I am* that *Love, loving.*

Exercise Your Spirit

(Read completely before you begin, pre-record,
or have someone else read to you as you do this exercise.)

Unconditional Love

Close your eyes and breathe in slowly and deeply until your body relaxes. As you relax, release all thoughts of anything . . . anyone . . . even yourself . . . and know that in this moment there is nothing you need to think about . . . no place you must go . . . nothing you need to do . . . Let yourself surrender to the freedom that is yours in this Sacred Space . . . If a thought occurs to you, let it drift away and dissolve into a wonderful white light . . . For the moment, call this Light *Unconditional* Love . . . Visualize the Light filling the room and breathe It in with every breath . . . deep into every cell, fiber, tissue, and organ of your body . . . Let the Light permeate every part of you . . . until the Light that is filling the room seems to be emanating from you and there is no separation between you and the room of Light . . . If there are others in the room, feel your oneness with them in the Light . . . feel yourself loving everyone in the room . . . without reason, judgment, or condition . . . The Light that is emanating from you feels Endless . . . and as you feel Its unlimited flow within you and pouring out from you, visualize the Light—this White Light that you are knowing as Unconditional Love—flowing out into the world . . . slowly . . . over your community . . .

country . . . across oceans . . . and continents . . . until the Light of Love emanating from you is circling the planet . . . Feel yourself loving the earth . . . every man, woman, child . . . every creature . . . every tree, mountain, meadow, ocean, stream . . . In all of the world there is only Love . . . the Love that you are . . . Love that life *Is* . . . Now see this Love flowing out into the Boundless Universe . . . as far out into Infinity as you can imagine . . . until there is no space where Unconditional Love is not . . . Now look into the White Light of Unconditional Love that is emanating from you and see if there are any dark spaces where up until now you have been believing that Unconditional Love was not present . . . in you or in another . . . Take your time . . . look closely and honestly . . . Now let the Light of Love flow into these spaces and see It eliminating the darkness just by being the Light . . . the White Light of Unconditional Love . . . the Love that you are . . . the Love that is *all* life.

When you feel complete with this exercise, open your eyes and immediately write down a word, phrase, or sentence that will help you to recognize Unconditional Love every moment, everywhere, between your prayers:

_____

_____

_____

_____

Peace

PEACE AS A QUALITY OF SPIRIT—the Peace we recognize in the first step of Spiritual Mind Treatment—is as Unconditional as the Love we recognize. It is not the peace we often seek between our prayers, for frequently we pursue a peace dependent upon the resolution of issues or a peace contingent upon a conversion of the opposition. To *seek* Peace is not the same as *being* Peace.

The Peace we recognize in Treatment is the Peace that *Is* in each moment, the Peace that flows through all life—in, above, beneath, and *as* creation—unimpeded by opposition, undisturbed by conflict, and unregulated by result. It is a Perfect Peace that is beyond analysis and consensus; a Peace that exceeds circumstance and condition; a Peace that is not contingent upon our personal conditions for Its existence. It is the Peace of God which "passes all understanding."[41] In our Treatments we recognize and declare that we live and move and have our being in *that* Peace which passes all understanding.

Because Peace is ever-present, we do not need to *seek* It between prayers nor set up outer conditions for Its appearance. All that is required in Treatment is our recognition of It. That same recognition is required between our prayers if we want to experience the harmonizing effects of Peace in all our affairs.

41. Philippians 4:7 (Lamsa)

When people and events appear disharmonious between our prayers, rather than recognizing Peace as the only Presence in spite of appearances, we frequently attempt to change the behavior, opinions, and attitudes of others in order for Peace to appear. Control, manipulation, coercion, and force become instruments of a peace that must be *achieved*. Recognition is the instrument of *that* Peace which already *Is*.

Throughout the ages the human race has attempted to bring about peace through war and conflict—both sides seeking to overpower their enemy, convert their opposition, and control the situation in order to achieve Peace. We might all agree that the horrors humankind has carried out against itself in the name of God are only surpassed by the battles it has waged in the name of Peace.

Though we personally may not agree with war and may feel that there are more *spiritual* ways to resolve social conflicts, between our prayers we may unconsciously hold the same points of view that beget war and violence, and in our daily life we may engage, mentally or verbally, in personal battles of our own.

When we bump up against the hardened assumptions of differing points of view between our prayers, we may not always recognize that Peace is the only Presence, and instead we may perceive differences as a sign of disunion. We might seek personal peace of mind through our attempts to convince others of the rightness of *our* position or the correctness of *our* way of doing things. Or perhaps between our prayers we might try to achieve peace by suppressing our own *true* nature and sense of what is right in order to appease another.

It is important for us to notice our patterns of belief and ask ourselves:

> *When something appears to go wrong, do I look for someone to blame before the situation can be resolved? Do I justify my temporary expressions of irritation, aggravation, and anger because of the behavior of others? Do I recognize Peace in every moment or do I look for a moment's peace?*

Between our prayers it is easy to feel separate from others and from Spirit. We look out through eyes that are framed in what feels like an isolated self and look into a world where diversity frequently appears to deny unity.

How often have we listened to the news, read a newspaper, or talked with a friend about the disharmony, violence, hate, and destruction in the world today and then shook our heads with a verbal "tsk-tsk" to emphasize how *different* the world is from us? But is it really possible for anyone to be completely different from the world when each of us is one with the world?

In our Treatments we affirm that we are One with Spirit and *all* of creation in heaven and on earth. The world that we see between our prayers *is* us, all of us, and individually and collectively we all affect its appearance with our every thought, word, and action.

There are no boundaries to Infinite Consciousness, but our individual experience of Peace is dependent solely upon our own awareness of It. The more we agree with what we see *out there*—or attempt to separate ourselves from what's out there out of fear—the more susceptible we are to the subconscious persuasions of the human race.

We ought not to allow ourselves to inadvertently accept the ideas of exterior, hostile, or evil forces in the world, for such acquiescence can pull us away from Peace and place us in harm's way.

If the subjective state of our thought creates our objective experience, and the subjective state of our thought is the sum total of our thinking and knowing, then we cannot afford to think "along a definite line of meditation for a specific purpose" that is engendered by fear and then walk out into the world of *our* creation. Our thoughts and words of doubt and fear, energized by the intensity of the feelings behind them, are as potently creative as our silent thoughts and spoken words about Peace in our prayers.

The Peace we claim as being at our "center" is not a place we must get to, but rather a moment-to-moment state of being from which we live. The Peace of God is not only the Center but is also the Circumference of our being—and Unconditional Peace requires nothing at all (not even a deep breath) for It to appear to us.

It may be easier for us to feel peaceful when we turn away from the chaotic objects of creation and turn to Pure, Formless Peace, but it is vital for us to remind ourselves that we are one with Peace—eyes open or eyes closed, in our quiet "centerings," in our silent meditations, when we speak our word in prayer, *and* when we speak our mind in the world.

When we recognize that Peace *Is* always—unchangeable and unfailing—we can feel It and express It no matter what, no matter where, because Peace is all there Is, and Peace is what we *already are.*

In the quietude of surrender, Peace appears, harmonizing discord, dissolving opposition, belying separation. In Peace, understanding celebrates diversity, compassion weaves unity. There is enchantment in the rising sun, comfort in its setting, tranquility in the repose of night. For Peace is What Is—*and I am* that *Peace, proclaiming.*

Exercise Your Spirit

(Read completely before you begin, pre-record,
or have someone else read to you as you do this exercise.)

Peace

Close your eyes and breathe in slowly and deeply until
your body relaxes. As you relax, release all thoughts of
anything . . . anyone . . . even yourself . . . and know
that in this moment there is nothing you need to
think about . . . no place you must go . . . nothing you
need to do . . . Let yourself surrender to the freedom
that is yours in this Sacred Space . . . If a thought
occurs to you let it drift away and dissolve into a wonderful blue light . . . For the moment call this Light
Peace . . . Visualize the Light filling the room and
breathe It in with every breath . . . deep into every cell,
fiber, tissue, and organ of your body . . . Let the Blue
Light of Peace permeate every part of you . . . until the
Light that is filling the room seems to be emanating
from you, and there is no separation between you and
the room of Blue Light . . . If there are others in the
room, feel your oneness with them in the Light . . .
feel the harmony and unity you share with them . . .
There is no opposition, no opposing opinion . . . yours
or theirs . . . There is only Peace and the unity of Peace
. . . The Light of Peace that is emanating from you
feels Limitless . . . and as you feel Its continuous flow
within you and pouring from you, visualize the

Light—this Blue Light that you are knowing as Perfect Peace—flowing out into the world . . . slowly . . . over your community . . . country . . . across oceans and continents . . . until the Blue Light of Peace emanating from you is circling the planet . . . Feel the earth at Peace . . . every man, woman, child . . . every race . . . every religion . . . every nation . . . In all of the world there is only Peace . . . the Peace that you are . . . the Peace that life *Is* . . . Now see this Peace flowing out into the Boundless Universe . . . as far out into Infinity as you can imagine. . .until there is no space where Peace is not . . . Now look into the Blue Light of Peace that is emanating from you and see if there are any dark spaces where up until now you have been believing that Peace was not present in you . . . in another . . . in the world . . . Take your time . . . look closely and honestly . . . Now let the Light of Peace flow into these spaces, eliminating the darkness just by being the Light . . . the Soft Blue Light of Peace . . . the Peace that you are . . . the Peace that is *all* life.

When you feel complete with this exercise, open your eyes and immediately write down a word, phrase, or sentence that will help you to recognize Peace every moment, everywhere, between your prayers:

_____

_____

_____

_____

Wisdom

IN THE FIRST STEP of Spiritual Mind Treatment we recognize only One Mind: the Mind of God. This Mind is All-knowing. It is Wisdom Itself. It is Infinite Mind originating unlimited ideas, the One Creator conceiving all of creation. It is the *only* Truth and the *only* Reality.

Though we often say that we align *our* mind with the One Mind, it is important for us to remember that *our* mind is always one with the One Mind because there is never our mind *and* the One Mind.

> *There is no such thing as your mind, my mind and God's Mind. There is only Mind, in which we all "live and move and have our being."* . . .
> *That which we call our subjective mind is, in reality, our identity in Infinite Mind.*[42]

Because the activity of *our* mind takes place in Infinite Mind, there is no limit to what we can know or conceive, no stopping-point for our thought or creativity, and no boundaries to our imagination. "It is impossible to plumb the depths of the individual mind, *because the individual mind is really not individual but is individualized.* Behind the individual is the Universal, which has no limits."[43]

Though in our Treatments we recognize the One

42. SOM 87.4, 6
43. SOM 30.2

Mind as the only Mind, between our prayers we are often tempted to view ourselves as mentally *on our own.* After all, our mind *feels* private and disconnected from others as well as from God. It doesn't feel "open to the Infinite." In fact, frequently it may not feel open to anything at all.

When we do not consistently recognize the Sacred Condition of our individual mind, between our prayers we frequently use *our* mind to engage in limited, negative, and fearful thinking, contemplating ideas and concepts that we would not consider appropriate or advisable in our Treatments. While we are lost in thought that is based upon a belief that our mind is not *always* one with Divine Mind, it is easy to forget the Power and Creativity that we are accessing with our every thought. Is it any surprise, then, that much of the time our life doesn't resemble our prayers?

We cannot fool Universal Mind by claiming the validity of a Truth in our prayers that we do not recognize in our day-to-day life. Our seemingly ineffective prayers are not due to the inadequacy of *our* mind as a vehicle for Truth or our failure to connect with the One Mind. *All* prayer is *answered,* and it is answered according to our thoughts and beliefs, in *and* out of prayer. "The riddle is solved, and we all use the creative power of the Universal Mind *every time we use our own mind."*[44]

If the Truth doesn't seem to have staying power in

44. SOM 30.2

our life, if It appears to come and go in our experience, it is because we have refused to completely release the old, habitual beliefs we hold in Mind and continue to speak and act from them.

All Wisdom is available to each of us as an individualization of the One Mind. We often limit our access to greater Wisdom by circumscribing and binding our mind with hardened, inflexible ideas and opinions. What we *think* we know often blocks what there *Is* to know. The world is filled with ideologies, isms, and schisms, with the righteous and the faithful in endless variety all believing that *their* truth is "truer."

But just as there is "no such thing as your mind, my mind, and God's Mind," there is no such thing as your truth, my truth, and God's Truth. There is that which we *believe* is true—and then there is Truth. Truth is *What Is* moment-to-moment.

We miss out on the greater experience of Truth because we are convinced that we already have the *correct* point of view. Everyone is certain that *their* way (or their interpretation of the guru's way, Allah's way, the Lord's way, or "Ernest's" way) is the *only* way. But as the old saying goes, once we think we know it all, there's nothing more we can learn.

The "V" in the Science of Mind symbol is open at the top to symbolize Unlimited Spirit descending through Substance into form. It could also be a symbol for the individual who is unceasingly open to the Truth.

> *For while it is true that we are immersed in an Infinite Intelligence, a Mind that knows all things, it is also true that this Intelligence can acquaint us with Its ideas only as we are able and willing to receive them. . . . Before It can reveal Its secrets, It must have an outlet. This outlet we shall be compelled to supply through our own receptive mentalities.*[45]

We cut Truth "off at the pass" when we adamantly insist that our truth is *the* Truth. It is only through our recognition of Something Greater, and our willingness to consciously maintain an opening for It, that Something New can reveal Itself in the moment. As Emerson so succinctly put it, we must get our "bloated nothingness out of the way" if we want True Light to be shed upon the issue at hand.

Our truth—our personal cumulative thoughts and experiences over time, religious and secular, and our inherited beliefs from the collective unconscious—and our persistence in holding onto our position prevent us from recognizing more of *What Is* in the moment.

A mind that believes itself separate from Spirit is not sufficient to the revelation of the Truth that awaits an open, unprejudiced mind that recognizes itself as one with the One.

45. SOM 40.1

In the still mind that silences the ego, quiets opin-ion, relinquishes estimations, Wisdom appears—Wisdom proclaiming, "I am"; Wisdom weaving Cosmos from chaos; Wisdom expressed as new thought, Wisdom manifested as cohesive action—for Wisdom is All that Is—and I am that Wisdom, expressing.

Exercise Your Spirit

(Read completely before you begin, pre-record,
or have someone else read to you as you do this exercise.)

Wisdom

Close your eyes and breathe in slowly and deeply, until your body relaxes. As you relax, release all thoughts of anything . . . anyone . . . even yourself . . . and know that in this moment there is nothing you need to think about . . . no place you must go . . . nothing you need to do . . . Let yourself surrender to the freedom that is yours in this Sacred Space . . . If a thought occurs to you, let it drift away and dissolve into a wonderful golden light . . . For the moment call this Light *Wisdom* . . . Visualize the Light filling the room and breathe It in with every breath . . . deep into every cell, fiber, tissue, and organ of your body . . . Let the Light of Wisdom permeate every part of you . . . until the Golden Light that is filling the room seems to be emanating from you, and there is no separation between you and the room of Light . . . If there are others in the room, feel your oneness with them in the Light . . . know that *all* that needs to known is already known among you . . . a shared Wisdom . . . a partnership of knowledge . . . relationship of Truth . . . The Light of Wisdom that is emanating from you feels beyond measure . . . and as you feel Its continuous flow within you and pouring from you, visualize the Light—this Golden Light that you are knowing as Wisdom—flowing out into the world . . . slowly . . . over your community . . . country . . . across oceans . . . and continents . . . until the Golden Light of Wisdom emanating from you is circling the planet . . . and know that Wisdom is guiding the planet . . . Wisdom is directing nature . . . Wisdom is orchestrating all phenomena . . . Wisdom is expressing through and as every man, woman, youth, child . . . every leader . . . every teacher . . . In all of the world there is only Wisdom . . . the Wisdom that you are . . . the Wisdom that life *Is* . . . Now see the Golden Light of Wisdom flowing out into the Boundless Universe . . . as far out into Infinity as you can imagine . . . until there is no space where Wisdom is not . . . Wisdom moving all the galaxies . . . every planet, star, comet, meteor . . . Now look into the Golden Light of Wisdom that is emanating from you and see if there are any dark spaces where up until now you have been believing that Wisdom was not present . . . in you . . . in another . . . in the world . . . Take your time . . . look closely and honestly . . . Now let the Light of Wisdom flow into these spaces eliminating the darkness just by being the Light . . . the Golden Light of Wisdom . . . the Wisdom that you are . . . the Wisdom that is *all* life.

When you feel complete with this exercise, open your eyes and immediately write down a word, phrase, or sentence that will help you to recognize Wisdom every moment, everywhere, between your prayers:

_____

_____

_____

_____

Wholeness

IN THE FIRST STEP of Spiritual Mind Treatment we often speak of Spirit as Being Whole—Complete, Perfect, Pure, Unadulterated—consummate in every quality; flawless in every form; infallible in every function. Within our Treatment we declare that *all* life proceeds from this One Perfect Cause.

We recognize that every form—from the smallest quantum unit to the largest universal structure—is engendered within the Wholeness of Spirit, and that "in spite of appearances" and behind such images as disease and dysfunction, Spiritual Perfection dwells. Such realization reveals to our consciousness a more perfect state of being for ourselves and others.

Spiritual Mind Treatment is a powerful healing agent and, as such, it is where we turn when we or others become ill, when conditions around us appear to be dysfunctional, and any time the Wholeness of Life we desire to experience appears divided, incomplete and imperfect.

Every now and then, however, we must all wonder why disease disappears and disharmonious situations harmonize as a result of our prayers, only to reappear as a different disease or another discordant situation for which we must pray once again. After all, if we are able to recognize the Perfect Presence of Spirit within us to the degree that a healing takes place, why don't disease, dysfunction, and disharmony disappear *permanently* from our experience?

Jesus said simply that it is done unto us as we believe, and it is important for us to remember that it is *done unto us* moment-to-moment, whether we're praying or not. One way or another, each of us "asks" for what we get. Sometimes our requests are intentional, other times they may be inadvertent, but either way what we experience *as* our life *perfectly* reflects what we believe life to be.

Frequently we soar the heights of spiritual recognition in our prayers and then open our eyes and fall back into the seeming reality of physical disease, dysfunction, and aging. We forget that our body continues to be "the word made flesh" between our prayers, that it remains the visible manifestation of Spirit, and that "body is always an *effect*, never a *cause*."[46]

We are tempted to perceive our body as having a life of its own, irrespective of our consciousness, with the capability of getting sick, old, and tired without our permission. Then, when we look at diseases in their dramatic and often grotesque shapes and forms clearly visible to our naked eye (or enlarged and detailed for us under a microscope), and when we hear scientific evidence that validates such terms as *incurable, fatal, terminal,* and *communicable,* we fear that the wholeness we affirmed in Treatment is reserved for

46. SOM 99.2

the context of prayer alone and not for the day-to-day *realities* of physical life.

When we think of our body as isolated and uninfluenced by our mind, our conversations and actions revolve around physical cause, prevention, and cure. We seek out vaccinations and medications to protect ourselves from the current bacterial, viral, or fungal infections. We look for the latest aids in slowing the downward tendencies of our body toward failing memory, inadequate energy, and recurring depression.

We forget that the Truth of our inviolate wholeness in prayer is true *between* our prayers. Truth is changeless. It doesn't vary with each *contagion nouveau*. The Wholeness of Life is Present in the jungle "hot spots" of viral and fungi mutations as well as in the hospitals of metropolitan civilizations.

The Truth can withstand the most potent biological weapons made by humankind. The Truth that healed the sick in the days of Jesus is the same Truth upon which we build our Treatments, and it is the same Truth of the whole, complete, and perfect nature of being upon which we can choose to base our daily life between prayers.

We shall never experience the true capabilities of our body if we continue to limit its function by habitual perceptions of its being isolated and uninfluenced by our mind and our thoughts and our words between prayers. We won't experience the longevity that our body might express if it were enlivened each moment by our recognition of our irrevocable oneness with the Power and Energy of the Universe. We won't experience the uninterrupted health that is *natural* to our body when it is vitalized each moment by our recognition of our unbroken connection with the Perfection of all life. We will not know what the *flesh* is intended to do until we are ready to do more than pray periodically to "fix what we've broken."

If we are able to formulate our thoughts into an effective course of meditation that leads us to a realization of wholeness when we sit down to pray *officially*, then we can do it when we are not praying, if we choose. If we were convinced in every moment that life is always expressing the Whole Being originating it, we would know beyond a shadow of a doubt that we could walk *through the valley of the shadow of death* and Truth would still be true—in us, through us, *as* us and all life.

God is All-in-all everywhere, in and out of prayer. Since the earth began, Truth has never failed those who have recognized Its Presence. It cannot fail—for the Whole, Complete and Perfect Life of Spirit is *What Is* in every moment, and there is none else.

In the quiet recognition of that Presence which invalidates deficiency, refutes dysfunction, and obliterates disunion, Whole, Complete and Perfect Being appears—Wholeness forming every part; Completeness pervading all existence; Perfection permeating all function. For the One Being is Whole—and I am that *Being, being.*

Exercise Your Spirit

*(Read completely before you begin, pre-record,
or have someone else read to you as you do this exercise.)*

Wholeness

Close your eyes and breathe in slowly and deeply until
your body relaxes. As you relax, release all thoughts of
anything . . . anyone . . . even yourself . . . and know
that in this moment there is nothing you need to
think about . . . no place you must go . . . nothing you
need to do . . . Let yourself surrender to the freedom
that is yours in this Sacred Space . . . If a thought
occurs to you let it drift away and dissolve into a wonderful green light . . . For the moment call this Light
Wholeness . . . Visualize the Light filling the room and
breathe It in with every breath . . . deep into every cell
. . . fiber . . . tissue . . . and organ of your body . . . Feel
the energy and vitality within the Light of Wholeness
. . . Let the Green Light permeate every part of
you...until the Light that is filling the room seems to
be emanating from you, and there is no separation
between you and the room of Green Light . . . If there
are others in the room, feel your oneness with them in
the Light . . . feel the health and vital energy you share
with them . . . There is no disease, no disability, no
aging . . . within yourself . . . within another . . . There
is only Wholeness and Perfection in each person, per-

fection in form, perfection in function . . . The Light of Wholeness that is emanating from you feels Inexhaustible . . . and as you feel Its continuous flow within you and pouring from you, visualize the Light—this Green Light that you are knowing as Wholeness—flowing out into the world . . . slowly . . . over your community . . . country . . . across oceans . . . and continents . . . until the Green Light of Wholeness emanating from you is circling the planet . . . Feel the health of the earth . . . the purity of its water and air . . . its pristine mountains and meadows . . . its unblemished cities and towns . . . every man, woman, child whole and vital . . . In all of the world there is only Wholeness . . . the Wholeness that you are, the Wholeness that life *Is* . . . Now see this Wholeness flowing out into the Boundless Universe . . . as far out into Infinity as you can imagine...until there is no space where Wholeness is not . . . Now look into the Green Light of Wholeness that is emanating from you and see if there are any dark spaces where up until now you have been believing that Wholeness was not present in you . . . in another . . . in the world . . . Take your time . . . look closely and honestly . . . Now let the Light of Wholeness flow into these spaces, eliminating the darkness just by being the Light . . . the Health-giving Green Light of Wholeness . . . the Wholeness that you are . . . the Wholeness that is *all* life.

When you feel complete with this exercise, open

your eyes and immediately write down a word, phrase, or sentence that will help you to recognize Wholeness every moment, everywhere, between your prayers:

_____

_____

_____

_____

Abundant Good

ABUNDANT GOOD IS A QUALITY of Spirit that is often recognized in the first step of Spiritual Mind Treatment. It is a recognition of God as Infinitely Good, and of Spirit as the One Unlimited Benefactor—the Source and Substance from which all life receives. "God is Spirit. Spirit is Substance and Substance is supply."[47]

It is *within* and *into* this Substance that we speak our word in prayer, confident that the treasures of the Spirit enrich and fulfill us, and that as much of the Kingdom of Heaven as we can embody is ours to experience.

In prayer, the idea of lack and limitation is nonexistent, for we realize that the boundless realm of imagination is a Universal storehouse that contains within It all that we could ever hope to bring forth into our experience.

Yet it seems that between our prayers, the perception of lack and limitation is difficult to release, given the appearances of impoverishment in the world and our own continued lack of sufficiency. We feel separate from the Abundant Life we claim in Treatment, as if we were *waiting for,* rather than *dwelling in,* the Abundant Life of Spirit. Frequently between our prayers we find ourselves depending upon worldly circumstances and events for our supply, rather than

47. SOM 262.3

upon the activity of Universal Creativity, and hoping that something will happen *to* us in the world rather than *through* us as the activity of Spirit.

When we believe that there are two things going on—the spiritual *and* the material, the Sacred *and* the mundane—it is easy to get caught up in appearances, and it is this dualistic perception of life that limits the good in our experience. We forget that our beliefs are acted upon *between* our prayers as well as in them, and that we are "setting a cause in motion" with our thoughts and words. We speak as if the Law of Universal Mind were inert in the space between our prayers and as if thoughts and words based upon lack and limitation were devoid of creative impulsion.

But every thought enters the Creative Realm. It is the sum total of our repetitive, habitual thoughts that creates the landscape of our life, and it is the cumulative beliefs we hold in mind that create prosperity, poverty, or mediocrity in our experience.

> *If I say, 'I am unhappy,' and continue to say it, the subconscious mind says, 'Yes, you are unhappy,' and keeps me unhappy as long as I say it, for thoughts are things, and an active thought will provide an active condition for good or evil. . . . Suppose one has thought poverty year after year, he has thereby personified a law which continues to perpetuate this condition.*[48]

48. SOM 118.3

We are self-perpetuating beings, replicating through the Universal Law of Mind our beliefs about ourselves and the world in our experiences. We are unlimited by nature and ever-creative in action. We cannot obstruct the creative nature of our thoughts between prayers; we can only *change our thinking.*

The world we see is our word made flesh—from cash on hand and food on the table to automobiles and recreational toys. Whatever we view as a prosperous life, and whether we are living that life or not, is the result of the sum total of our thinking. *Everything* that is seen is made from the Substance of that which is Unseen, no matter how it appears in our life.

If we believe that thought causes *anything,* then we must also believe that thought causes *everything.* Our outer financial circumstances are the result of our inner perceptions.

> *The Spiritual world is the CAUSE of the material; we are spiritual beings governed by mental law.*[49]

> *The conviction that heals is that God is all in all and that there is no material cause or effect.*[50]

It is important for us to remember that whether we pray for financial increase or work for it, earn it in dividends, or win it in the lottery, it is born of conscious-

49. SOM 448.1
50. SOM 413.5

ness and ultimately "God-ordained," for nothing is separate from Spirit, and Spirit is Unlimited in expression. We need only look around us. The abundance of life is everywhere (there are over 3,500 varieties of mushrooms alone!).

If our mind is full of thoughts of lack and we constantly speak of what we don't have or can't do, how can we expect our life to improve? If we focus on our losses, if our declarations are of life's unfairness, if we worry about getting more or what might be taken from us, then our Good is forced to squeeze through the tiny apertures we give It in our consciousness. What we think about and speak of between our prayers reveals or conceals the Truth about which we have prayed.

We cannot turn to Spirit periodically and then perceive our life as separate from It the rest of the time, and then hope to experience the prosperity we have affirmed in prayer. In fact, because of the tendency of Divine Substance to continuously create through our beliefs and concepts, our life is in danger of even further depletion. "For to him who has shall be given and it shall increase to him; but to him who has not, even that which he has shall be taken away from him."[51]

Our thoughts and words increase upon themselves, adding to our experiences according to our beliefs. Just as in mathematics negative two (-2) plus negative two becomes negative four (-4), our *negative* concepts of

51. Matthew 13:12 (Lamsa)

lack and limitation based upon our belief in a life separate from Spirit *add up* and manifest as less and less
in our lives.

From the smallest to the greatest forms, Life
expresses Itself in Abundance. It is all good, Abun-
dantly Good, for God is All-in-all.

> *This is the keynote to a realization of the more
> abundant life, to the demonstration of success in
> financial matters. . . . To bring a realization of
> the Presence of the Spirit into all our acts is to
> prove that God is all—even in the slightest things
> which we undertake.*[52]

---

52. SOM 262.3, 263.1

In the Pure Emptiness of that Presence which satiates desire, eliminates hunger, and extinguishes longing, Abundant Good appears— Unlimited Source nourishing all life; Boundless Joy fulfilling the heart; Infinite Substance supplying endless good. For Good is all there Is— *and I am* that *Good, manifesting.*

Exercise Your Spirit

(Read completely before you begin, pre-record,
or have someone else read to you as you do this exercise.)

Abundant Good

Close your eyes and breathe in slowly and deeply until your body relaxes. As you relax, release all thoughts of anything . . . anyone . . . even yourself . . . and know that in this moment there is nothing you need to think about . . . no place you must go . . . nothing you need to do . . . Let yourself surrender to the freedom that is yours in this Sacred Space . . . If a thought occurs to you, let it drift away and dissolve into a wonderful prism of light . . . For the moment, call this radiant, multicolored Light *Abundant* Good . . . Visualize the Light filling the room and breathe It in with every breath . . . deep into every cell, fiber, tissue, and organ of your body . . . Let the rainbow of Light permeate every part of you...until the Light that is filling the room seems to be emanating from you, and there is no separation between you and the room of Colorful Light . . . If there are others in the room, feel your oneness with them in the Light . . . feel the fulfillment and joy that you share with them . . . There is no lack . . . no wanting . . . no emptiness . . . within yourself or anyone else . . . There is only Abundant Good within the multitude of colors of Light . . . The

Light that is emanating from you feels Full yet Boundless . . . and as you feel Its continuous flow within you and pouring from you, visualize the Light—this beautiful prism of Light that you are knowing as Abundant Good—flowing out into the world . . . slowly . . . over your community . . . country . . . across oceans . . . and continents . . . until the Light of Abundant Good emanating from you is circling the planet in endless colors . . . Feel the fullness of the earth . . . the oceans and rivers teeming with life . . . the mountains and meadows carpeted with beauty . . . every man, woman, child fulfilled . . . every heart's desire met . . . every being enriched . . . sufficient in all things . . . every imagination consumed with the joy of Good . . . In all of the world there is only Abundant Good . . . the Abundant Good that you are . . . the Abundant Good that life Is . . . Now see color-filled Light flowing out into the Boundless Universe . . . as far out into Infinity as you can imagine . . . until there is no space where Abundant Good is not . . . Now look into the prism of the Light of Abundant Good that is emanating from you and see if there are any dark spaces where up until now you have been believing that Abundant Good was not present in you . . . another . . . in the world . . . Take your time . . . look closely and honestly . . . Now let the Rainbow of Light that is Abundant Good flow into these spaces, eliminating the darkness just by being the

Light . . . the Radiant Light of Abundant Good . . . the Abundant Good that you are . . . the Abundant Good that is *all* life.

When you feel complete with this exercise, open your eyes and immediately write down a word, phrase, or sentence that will help you to recognize Abundant Good every moment, everywhere, between your prayers:

_____

_____

_____

_____

*The author welcomes questions and comments
related to this book.*

E-mail: SacredContinuum@aol.com